MW01472456

HYMN

Also by John Barton

Poetry

A Poor Photographer
Hidden Structure
West of Darkness
Great Men
Notes Toward a Family Tree
Designs from the Interior
Sweet Ellipsis
Hypothesis

Poetry Chapbooks

Destinations, Leaving the Map
Oxygen
Shroud
Runoff
Asymmetries (In the House of the Present and *The Strata)*

Editor

Silences
belles lettres / beautiful letters
We All Begin in a Little Magazine: Arc *and the Promise of Canada's Poets, 1978–1998* (with Rita Donovan)
Seminal: The Anthology of Canada's Gay Male Poets (with Billeh Nickerson)

HYMN
John Barton

Brick Books

Library and Archives Canada Cataloguing in Publication

Barton, John, 1957–
Hymn / John Barton.

Poems.
ISBN 978-1-894078-76-4

I. Title.

PS8553.A78H94 2009   C811'.54   C2009-902314-8

Copyright © John Barton, 2009
Second Printing – November 2010

We acknowledge the Canada Council for the Arts, the Government of Canada through the Book Publishing Industry Development Program (BPIDP), and the Ontario Arts Council for their support of our publishing program.

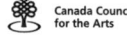

Canada Council for the Arts   Conseil des Arts du Canada   Canada   ONTARIO ARTS COUNCIL / CONSEIL DES ARTS DE L'ONTARIO

The cover painting is by Attila Richard Lukacs: *Three Boys*, mixed media on canvas, 54" X 44.5", 1998.

The author photograph was taken by Diana Tegenkamp.

The book is set in City BQ and Sabon.

Design and layout by Alan Siu.

Printed and bound by Sunville Printco Inc.

Brick Books
431 Boler Road, Box 20081
London, Ontario N6K 4G6

www.brickbooks.ca

In memory of my father

Men yearn for poetry, though they may not confess it...
—E. M. Forster

Contents

I

Aide-Mémoire   13

II IDEOGRAMS

This Cabinet   19
Caught in the Updraft   20
The Piano   22
Ideogram, in the Half-Light   23
Free Associations   24
Geology of the Body   29
Persona   30
Shopping at Capers   33
Hallelujah   35
Inwards   36
Pathetic Fallacy   37
Le Tombeau de Sylvia Plath   39
Installation in Homage to Gathie Falk   41
Foul Bay at 2 AM   42
Anxiety   43
Frieze   44
Aquarium   46
Saumon Fumé   47
On Evia   49
This Land Is Our Land   52
Runoff   53

III NARRATIONS

In the House of the Present   57

The Strata   60

Sombrio Beach   70

The Troubles   71

Asymmetries   75

IV HYMNS

Excerpt from a Travel Journal   83

Eros   85

Him   86

10 Lines for X   87

Way Finding   88

Fucking the Minotaur   91

Man of Your Dreams   92

Our Embrace: Random Études, 1 Through 4

   Pastoral   93

   Divertissement   94

   Pastiche   95

   Caprice   96

Warhol   98

Portal   100

A Boys' Own, with Queen   102

Sandy Hill Gothic   104

Hymn   105
Amnesia   107
Days of 2004, Days of Cavafy   109
The Afterlife   116

V

Polygonics   121

Acknowledgements   124

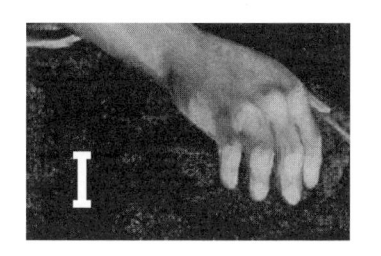

I

Aide-Mémoire

First there was the dancer

        then the refugee

                then the gambler

and, counting back

wards at random, the anaesthetist

the adjuster, the interior designer known for

his way with gilt and feathers, the former military

adviser who still liked to trail men undercover followed

by the TV actor whose agent died afraid he would contract AIDS

the librarian who collated records about his lovers into alphanumeric

order (access points being size and chat name only), including Scam, the squeegee

boy with goose-fleshed skin who reeked of WINDEX, and Time-Lapse, the photographer whose life

blurred beyond the focused alchemic subtleties of black and white

unlike the lobbyist who remained uniformly shameless

or the statistician who was so neutral about

those he loved, he seemed no

more than average

so I left him for the substitute

teacher who set such a teaser of a quiz
I could not resist him, the choices so multiple
the possibilities for love were endless, or so I thought, exhausting

his pre-scored answers far too quickly
unwrapping the Eskimo
sandwich

the DICKIE DEE
ice cream kid sold me after
he quit my bed and dressed, he too was looking
for a father figure, someone to sleep with who makes him

feel safe

another literary man like me but perhaps one
more famous, who might read *The Odyssey* aloud to him in bed
before lights out, only to let us undock from our aimless, common moorings

I am the homeless man, *hypocrite lecteur*
you long to take in

who owns no baggage to pack yours into
who always needs a shower, my shoulders especially broad and dirty
with a back it takes hours to wash, who will slip on your sweaty CALVIN KLEINS

14

afterwards, if you want, and then let you peel them off, who will stay
for another night or another lifetime even if you don't
ask nicely, men are so
fidèle
je me souviens, I am
the one you recognize
from the bar who looks nervously away, the one
you confront when shaving, the peculiarities of your face hard
to summarize in the clipped, forever-young vocabulary of the companion ads, you are

    the Winged Victory   a Herb Ritts photo   Antonio Banderas

Tom of Finland   you are negative capability   the lineman for the county

the towel boy at the baths   you are Alexander the Great

    Dennis Cooper   the stocker at Loblaws   Dr Jekyll

you are PRESIDENT'S CHOICE   the objective correlative

you are

the man in chinos at the street corner with a broken umbrella
your wet BROOKS BROTHERS shirt unbuttoned
at the neck, whom I

hesitate to give

directions, whose reflection
is trampled by the rainy afternoon
crowds of a city where no one ever truly lives.

II
IDEOGRAMS

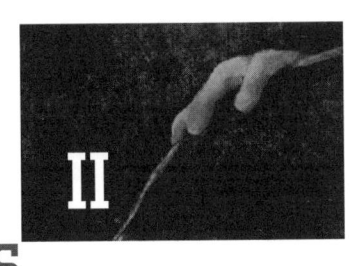

This Cabinet

locks from the inside

its key on twine looped
round my neck
cold jagged teeth burning

into pale skin.

It is pre-dawn.
Shadows
the trees cast over pink and fading

snow are antlers

about to be shed, elk
stooping to
drink from the thawing lake.

Ice porous as lace
edges the mossy shore, cracks

to the touch, melts

on my tongue, sluice heady
with spruce and as cold

as pickerel, weak late
winter sun at last
burning

a keyhole through low
thinning cloud.

Caught in the Updraft

> *A kite is the last poem you have written...*
> —Leonard Cohen

What do you say about a boy who flies

his sister's shoes at the end of a kite
vaulting above an empty field, leaving her

stranded on a patch of grass nosing through
thin sheets of runoff, too many wavelets

fracturing a mirror of scattering, scudding
cumulus for her to stop

kissing her boyfriend, the wind keeping her kid
brother busy—where it comes from no

one can guess, the gusts this March warm and inspired
fast as a gazelle across some distant plain he starts

hunting as he leans back in shirtsleeves, the kite
ruddered by shoes open-toed and strung up

higher than he could have hoped for, the jubilant
tail of the kite almost valedictory, so tiny everything

seems now, his sister and her boyfriend lost
to him on their eyelet of grass turning

green and tender early in the season
snow-melt enticing silt from the mountains

all around them, both unconcerned whole geologic
ages could pass in an hour, the water isolating

them in the field already quick with micro
organisms still no more than ideas

wriggly with possibilities so limitless
his knees unlock against their pull, the far-off

glaciers a constant glimpsed as if
through dawn curtains upon waking, love

a variable he will have a hard time
believing can be proved, the tug on

the line beyond reason, any word almost
lifting him off his feet, the impurity

of its drive anarchic, spontaneous, a fast one
he will spend unutterable lifetimes failing

to control, his sister's shoes an anchor
the wind is there for, so many

kites in his head to sweet-talk into the sky
his hands becoming rope-burned

and cagey, he can't see himself
wanting anyone's

help?

The Piano

It was something you would never let me play, the unseen body
of its music never to be drawn out by my fingers, its keys still

tantalizing, just beyond reach, sheet music ready on a stand, time
signature dark as the sheen of its hinged lid, a rich and luminous

eggplant dozing past twilight in a garden you've kept to yourself
this upright locked in the study, its shape reserved for your touch

feet working the pedals, a pilot snug in the cockpit of your Phantom
—you fathered me after the war—such a nightfighter high above

us all, high above our dreaming suburb, speed and ascent scored
across the clouds' wind-shred staff—what bruises, what passion

leafing out, vines climbing into indigo skies, the unpicked glories
of your music open, camouflaged by the bass notes of its engines.

Ideogram, in the Half-Light

You are sleeping, the alarm yet to rouse you, and I am

afraid it will disturb us with its aimless news, your body
turning away from me, shoulders curved against the sweet

half-light of darkness in the first room we share, early sun
sliding through thin hotel curtains across our bed, traffic

rising, warm air lifting from the drowsy city floors below
—dreaming: shock of the elevator shaft, of storey collapsing

into story, you and I; who am I, talking in your sleep, you begin
to tell me, words wearing down in the radiance of descending

inwards—psyche—beyond the radio alarm, the news I cannot
turn off, digital time altering place, integers cutting through

whatever quiet you may well harbour, my fingers settling
on your lips, analogue and anodyne, keys to an unspoken-for

country, feathers from my pillow your involuntary breaths
might blow off, patient dreamer sleeping through the fearful

the courage to love, the blades of your shoulders parentheses
against my chest while the zero news, the alarm, outdistance

this drifting, unwritten hour—sweet man, when my time
has come and the elevator doors stutter somewhere open

wake me gently: you are sleeping, you are my sleeping form.

Free Associations

i

I write "Charleswood."
You rewrite "Small trees."

I think "Vacancy."
Untouched land.

Caragana.
Yellow bits of news

print crumpling among
bushes in a vestigial

lot.
Blind

Man's Bluff.
Such shady trees.

Nose Hill bald
with dusk overshadowing

games of tag. The pause.
Five years old.

Crepuscular prairie
remnant impinged upon

by suburbs, the last
crocus and dirt

under a man's fingernails
while another

house goes
up, small

trees bull
dozed, the cut and lashed

boughs, my green
scavenged bones hung in

side a tent of uninflated
skin—temporary

shelter (something felt if
untouched) sagging

with dry
short-grass light.

ii

I cross out "Grass."
You re-enter "Small trees."

Disoriented
by the familiar

by the suburb's fixed streets
I unfold

a map across the convalescent wastes
of my desk.

Highway 1A.
Cochrane. Ghost Lake. Jumping Pound. Exshaw. Banff.

One word leading beyond the other.
The clouded

edge of the mountains ripping
open, air jagged

and jangly at the prospect
of sun, the welcome lonely paddle

stroke through the apparent
pink opaque

shallows of the Vermillion Lakes.
But first the meandering

anxious track.
What it carries treeless

climbing above the mind's freak
constructions and bypass.

Carnal solitude captured
inside its windsock of weather.

This unnecessary
highway, its denuded story I am

destined to wear
all my life.

iii

I underscore "Unnecessary."
You italicize "Small trees."

How they bud out in metaphors overnight
roots sinking down, not just through

the body where, ravenous
they extend idle

bits of consciousness, slyly absorbing
the absent rains—

but into the heart
its dusty

lots primed for sub
division with transplanted

shade trying to suck
dry the inevitable

grid of desire.
Driving west, the gradual

mountains in the distance are gradually
mountains and, against intelligent

design, are release
made flesh from the first

memory on:
a lineman high up

beneath the chinook arch
wind vibrating

wires he threads live through
icy glass insulators.

Prehistories of standing
alone, struck still

at my bedroom window.
The stripped

streets of Charleswood
cool to metaphors

stencilled despite
themselves to leaf

out below him before
the thawing white

shadows of peaks
incandescent

in the premature
spring sun.

Geology of the Body

Unceasing how the planet renews itself—
   landforms shift, plate frictioning

against plate, restless
   mountains reared up under pressure along fault

lines while oceans rise, storm-boiled
   glacial bodies you navigate, mapping the rivers

siphoned into them, sweat pooling in the hollows
   along your collarbone while you work

things out, the exhilarations
   of discovery counterbalanced by the weight

you lift above your head, shoulders, thighs
   and back hardened with time into fundament

apparently immutable, your chest the breastplate
   of a continent behind which your heart is

free to swim in its landlocked sea of opiates
   the planet rescued from the inattentions

of a brain too mindful of the soft
   rich clay housing it, of all that is ground

down and mixed into a grey amalgam
   and spread, muddy blood-warm shallows

across which our ancestors stray, recently
   erect, marking you with indifferent footprints.

Persona

This voice
how it breaks

into lines, regulated
by breaths my body

sets
irregular

expansive—
filling and filled

by unstable margins
of pressure, the sweet

sage-slick mirages
of heat forever at arm's

length as the pickup I am
driving evaporates into

the dusk-backlit haphazard
first hills, climbing

towards harvest-glowing aspens
up channels of clear

cut paving the way, lofty
words condensing

into perpetually
broken

white lines
hiving off futures

that, with the brights on
buzz distractedly

past while what we approach
approaches without

sign through the darkness
however light my foot

to the gas, through
certain personal

landscapes, the brakes
sly, eurhythmic, syllabic.

No question of
who is

speaking, my friend
my stranger, the dis

location between what I
say and what you

hear, androgynous
sited in some

invisible wilderness best
left on its own

to explore us, who remain
so much more than

the sum of the usual
equations thrown

open to the night.
Something speaks unscripted

from behind this scrub
of shadow and exhaust, fellow

ventriloquist, illusive
member of the choir, you

hitched this
ride with me, the physiology

of highway inflected
and now gearing

down through your body as it
tunnels through mine, its western

terminus
the provisional end of

all lines, open
to interpretation—

laconic
cordilleran—

Shopping at Capers

For you: Spartan, Golden
Newton, and Gala, unsprayed

unfenced-in, mouth-watering
light from the Gulf Islands.

Sea salt buffs off
on your hands, apples

smooth-chested and slick
licked by the clean

air they hang into, loading
branches as they fatten

pendulous, another and another
cupping into your palm.

For me: kiwi, furred
and rubbed, tinder

against my fingertips
a not-slow burn, thunder

eggs blown sky-high past
the azure and broken open

distillate halves
of the heart laid bare, *yes*

and *yes,* tart cabochons
of peridot icing my tongue.

For us: our bodies
and their unpredicted

seismic recoveries.
You've eased beneath

me, the Juan de Fuca plate
remote islands disappearing

coastal ranges shaken awake.
Orchards harvested

by aftershocks, windfalls
bruised and unbruised

sold not far from where
we live, homeward-bound

shopping bags heavy
with foretastes of twilight.

Hallelujah

The flesh inside this orange is viscera until I ease off
the rind, scrape away with bitten nails the pith hanging

down in strings from wedges ripped free, the tang rich
and dangerous, cold-water fusion eating into the lining

of my cheek, afterglow florescent in my gut—praise
condensing on trees, picked half-ripe, crate-packed

for the journey northwards into my frozen country
friction of skin jostling skin, angst mellowed away

as a driver pushes deeper overnight beyond melting
mountains in Vermont, temptation skidding past

jolts and swerves in the road, my half-life caught
in the balance as I weigh another dozen, each wedge

the ticklish imprint of your testes salting my tongue
the intent of shed linen trousers and Panama hats

of swimmers run amok riding the surf at Key West
coiled inside every envelope of nectar we swallow—

blood oranges, tangerines, clementines, mimosas
—you peel them fast; sleek they slip down my throat.

Inwards

Among the dwarf carnations you brought me: a cutting

with two buds, a flame snaring them while we sit outlined
in candlelight shed against the window, the vase cool

burning to the touch as late winter frost, the charred petals
brittle flakes of blood suspended among reviving blooms

fed on sugared water by jointed stems, shy crinolines red
edged and open. This is the week's arrangement, brooding

at the centre of a table we are drawn to, where platefuls
remain unfinished, words seared by anger, others served

when cold, but with an aftertaste to make us hunger
patinas of salt flaming the tongue, why else chew over

so many meals? Not because love incinerates the brain
with a radiance of flowers burning. No, it opens inwards

the path ahead sentinel as lit windows seen from far off.

Pathetic Fallacy

Annuals hardly ever endure our season, your hothouse seedlings
flirtatious and sickly as orphaned puppies, pot-bound when bedded

in shallow-raked, frost-straitened loam, its substrates an untutored
coalescence of sand and clay, the exposures seldom wholly felt

through—unimaginable light, watery uncertainties—all succulents
too tender for my very shivery Laurentian environs, moon-shaped

leaves straggling southwards, the stems anxiously moored
elongated and pale, the roots grasping at the errant nutrients

for a week's wild efflorescence, a racket of colour and scent
to arrest my attention, your gardening shears poised and a bud

vase washed when every gaping flower, just as suddenly, drops
seed—*how we persist in forced metaphor*—sun-drunk sepal losing

wet petals to the wind while our backs are turned, the thin limp
wristed stalks dying down into the rot-rich earth under snows

blown in from Alberta, evolution's appetite for deviation coiled
slackly inside those amnesiac seeds you aim into next year's bed

pathetic fallacy a trope for our phallocentrism, your scattered
penchant for feyly manicured blooms in contrast to my hardy

weediness, desire's other phylum, so perennial and wayward
in its rank cupidity, a network of thickening stems subversively

spread and prone to survive winters underground, unrepentant
and visceral, tenacious and wily, though you have tried hard

to eradicate its hold on my ground, challenging the rapaciousness
indigenous to this landscape, how it thrives in overworked soil

your poisons and admonishments, the civics of a carebound society
no match for the male body, the varieties of love it husbands

with rampant stoicism, anthurium and goldenrod, flamboyant
and irritating rivals unnaturally adversarial, the aggression

of their beauty soul-destroying to those who stand forbidden
to harvest them, who, unrequited, must bear their flourish

and wane, annual or perennial, domestic or weed, the bees
of the open field the final impartial terrorists, our bodies

at last sensing of their own accord exactly when the time is
ripe for stressed earth to lie fallow, *leaving the language to be.*

Le Tombeau de Sylvia Plath

How long have we stood here gazing blankly into the muddy yellow
Yorkshire clay where against your wishes you have lain, a citizen

of your own century even in death, with nothing much left beyond
a loosening paradigm of bones to claim you with, fugitive wisps
of blonde hair or an effaced piece of heirloom jewellery a cousin might
recollect, a watch stopped not long after no one could hear it stop.

There are strangers who come here who cannot shake the apparition
of you faintly smiling, perfection betrayed if satisfied, a smile they try on

in the mirror before leaving for the graveyard with narcissus, perhaps tulips
or poppies—your studied moods symbolized—to stand and conjecture
over that other grave, the words, tease your last breaths from them only
as they can be surmised, head poised in the oven on an ironed napkin

at 23 Fitzroy Road, Yeats' subdivided house the perfect dark address
you had hoped to fortify with wine and laughter to give you strength

poetry a gas jet you woke up to one morning in February, as always
but finally could not light, lungs filling with an inspiration so terrible
you would not write it out, the only accolade you could welcome
was its odourless embrace *hello, goodbye*. How we keep reviving

the body of your work to enjoy an unstable place in our book-lined lives
keep taking it down from the shelf, trained by our literate scruples only.

You have fallen a long way, you were right, and not into the rocky earth
of your beloved Devon among the anchoring roots of a familiar yew tree
as you had hoped, to be sheltered from a weather you need no longer feel.
Instead you lie far from home, far from Massachusetts and the woman

you have become, no less hallowed than stone men exhumed from bogs
in Europe, their agonies tested, the facts suggested by the unspeakable

mouths and strangely passionate eyes hollowed by silt. Be glad of your final
loss of consciousness, a nightmare without ears the living are loathe to ride.
I wait by your grave in the rain, firmly in the footsteps of all the others who want
to commune with the dead for no reason, yellow clay encumbering my shoes.

I have even brought you roses, the adulterous buds affecting to be full-blown.
I wanted to believe in tenderness, but our age is not tender; there is no tender age.

Installation in Homage to Gathie Falk

on the picket line, National Gallery of Canada, May 2001

Red shoes leading us forward, the porcelain-smooth leather dyed and the red not
dying, the efflorescence of sunset flushed through storm clouds glazed overhead

withholding the evaporated red rain of Belarus the wind blew west from Chernobyl
refugees for centuries walking westward in red shoes turned black in the news

reels our parents watched after the whitest of nightly air raids during the darkest
of days brought to mind by red shoes lined up in single file down a municipal sidewalk

the shed shoes of Auschwitz or those removed before dance class, pairs of unbound
feet called up to the barre, faces turned forward and looking *en pointe* into the blood

shot depths of the eye, red shoes leading past insomnia or hallucination to stare
down forethought and aftermath, power meant to be balanced and binary, hand

linked with hand rather than toe stepping on toe, the shoes we slip back into
forced to walk in circles around the public square outside the closed museum

where the shoes insist we belong, blood coursing in our interlocking veins, red
shoes leading us forward, umbrellas opening as one against the corrosive rain.

Foul Bay at 2 AM

Soundlessly the clam diggers flicker down stairs hanging
   against grey cliffs sunk low into ebb tide, lamps strapped

to hard hats as they descend in procession, holy miners
   of night, the only noise a tingle of spades inside

empty steel pails, a flinty inner echo of quiet, the wind's
   sandpaper lifting mist from the sky, starlight flinted

against the moon's albino, half-shut eye, clam diggers walking
   into the sea, the stars soluble, phosphorescent, unclaimed.

Anxiety

Before I broke the window I was always on the inside looking out
—words excised from a notebook, ignored till now, till I look out

a window at this time of year, cracked panes jangling in the frame
the frame itself jarred by the first cold wind to lift from the river

winter oppressing me on schedule as it always does, these words
flags snapping at the Turkish embassy two doors down, twigs

fragmenting in the cold, the first shattered crimson leaves already
below my window, my shadow from this lit room anticipating

war, in Kurdistan perhaps, darkness cast across the premature snow.
Before I broke the window I was always on the inside looking out

thinking I had inside knowledge, thinking I had something special
or nothing much to say about how to change the way things were

words cutting my wrist as I broke through the pane with my fist
instant shards lodging self-doubt below the skin, and numbness.

Every window that window. The anxiety. The severed nerve.
The river below exposed as a throat, its argentine integument

taut as a sail resonant with storm, dark clouds of algae flying to
the surface, mottled imperfections swirling into whatever ripens

and gets reflected back, my eyes never once clear and undisturbed.
A child face down in snow in Kurdistan, blood pouring from his mouth.

Before I broke the window I was always on the inside looking out
nothing admitted in until the airless seasonal rage of the unloved

lacerated my solitude with sudden subconscious force, the numb
reality of wind. If I could, in my arms I would gather up that child

and run for cover across every artificial border, these words
I cannot forget, impossible bandages for his mortal wounds.

Frieze

Sometimes the body
loses
      grasp of its vocabulary, awkward

among trees reaching
           upwards, mimicking
                          grace.
Snow falls into
      night, heart
valves closing, unvalued

and cold, the mute branches of the remaining

boulevard elms weighed down, unable

to break
      the persistent drifting
           with time, mattering
                        less.
Days shorten, narratives
      erase, the toboggan
hill ridden clean of all tracks.
The street through

the park cuts deeply, unsettling shadows
                swerving
a stray white
      somnambulant
           fox insinuating
                  its frost
flecked tail of twitching
      fathomless
           stars orbited by traces
of other
improbable worlds.

Unnavigable constellations.

Headlamps of random traffic quiescent behind mist.

Inaccessible viscera.
                    The cortex uneasy
                                        in the space
time of sullen accumulation.
                            The disembodied
corporeal
shimmer of the bearded

streetlights tightening inside as I swallow

back silences
                if voiced   freeze
                                        in the untracked
air
        (white and grammarless—

Aquarium

At night, under the river, there are rooms, doors opening and closing
in the chill arrhythmic currents, all of us floating. Who really lives

down here, windows opening and closing, doors ajar? Our dead
shoaled in rent-controlled apartments just under the surface, the river

on edge, held back by its relentless slow moving. It is almost winter
a luminous quartz despite the eddies' slick tongue and anaesthetic lips

the incantatory snows a shift into freezing rain drawn close as a cloud
of falling, crystallizing mayflies, of kisses, only to melt, and we are fish

ignoring hunger in these overpopulated, cold-blooded shallows, busy
starving while we explore picaresque many-roomed castles of garbage

gills filtering out remnants of oxygen, tiny mouths nipping ragged
moons out of the mirror throwing dark reflections of the narcissistic

trees back at themselves, they deserve it, feckless anglers with baited
roots. In the high-rises where we sleep, our bodies open and close

approximate absence, recasting nervous lines into how we came
to be down here, why we have yet to crawl out, sudden humans

gutted after such a haunted swim through darkness, so empty come
daybreak we long for our familiars—the dogfish and the lamprey.

Saumon Fumé

Whoever translated the menu
at Angeline in Les Galleries Lafayette

did so badly, there's no escaping
the aftertaste of his words in my mouth

as if they were in the mouth of another
my heart giddy and dissociate—

"smocked salmon" *à la carte*...
—an epiphany perhaps, but not

the food of love, instead a net full
of this year's declining catch

stood atwirl on their tailfins
the best of their generation lined up

and looking quite fetching in frilled
aprons with bibs smocked

by my mother whose hand also
stitched them for my sisters and no

doubt for me, costumed in drag
before I had any taste, foretelling

in habit what I—like these mincing
fish—am proficient at: kicking

up my heels in some nicotine-rank
torch-song bistro in the Marais

assuming the fishy body
language of this sleek chorus line

their flesh not yet terminally infused
with smoke before they doff

aprons into the ravenous arms
of the audience to swim upstream

in the buff into the highlands
virile bodies tattered by rocks

skin hanging away in strips
the teeming whitewater rouged

up as sunset or sunburn—more in
common with sharks at a bathhouse

these frowsy crepuscular doyennes
than the pretty-headed torpedos

of svelte with quick-fire payloads
they once were—prematurely

aged by the journey backwards
to the source, which is not

the destiny of anything kissable
and where they elect not to

spawn, but spill their DNA
unregenerate onto the stream's

bed of gravel, together or alone
for the hell of it, kamikaze

and correct in whatever language
however battered by love—

On Evia

If so little remains, how can I
  remember, remember our dizzying

Descent on foot along the stream, eyes
  roaring step after step over steep

Slippery pitched slabs of marble littered
  with petals, red petals on white laid down

Wet by sauna-hot breezes blown out
  from quarries the Romans emptied, this

Marble prized above all others, barged from
  Karystos to the limits of the map they drew

Our psychic map—I too have hiked beyond
  twelve columns at rest on a windswept

Mountain across the valley as it tumbles
  towards the Aegean past a ruined

Venetian fortress, columns left lying as they
  fell by slaves no governor could recall

From some antique war, my servitude
  their servitude inexorably squandered

Karystostine marble recut, polished, set
  in basilicas and spas from Westminster

To Sidon, local streets cobbled anew
  while water falls sunlit and shadowed

Sonorous over veins of calcite exposed under
  plane trees and chestnuts as we scramble

Past the terraces of descending pools full
   and empty, empty and so full, moist

Spikes of oleander, sprays of peony, orchids
   coiled in spongy undergrowth, haze

Ghosting the path ahead to beaches unfurled
   against the surf washing up at Kalliani

Azure without sea floor, hot buoyant
   skin seared in riffled sweeps of frigid salt

Goats astride branches of coast-side
   olives above sheep we push through

In the hundreds as we climb down
   from the dragon houses crowning

Mount Ochi—what sunburnt rites broke
   off upholding the tumbledown roofs

None can guess, snaking past long
   deified Byzantine hillside chapels cut

Into the dimmed gorge, faint light
   fluid and cool to our lips, thousands

Of bells pinging around bent grazing
   heads, an ancient asynchronous new

Age music the sheep are unattuned to
   as they browse rattling grasses

And low branches, air weightless, tinny
   in descant behind us, alert shards

Of marble plinking sharps under
   foot as everything slides after

Us to the sea in a jumble, mnemonics
   of the stream we trace our way

Along never about to run dry even
   in summer, Karystos catching eternities

Of hearsay inside a net its taverna-lined
   streets dip towards the reflective

Clear harbour, on Evia, where islanded
   I am a visitor visiting no longer.

This Land Is Our Land

How I love to hold yours while you pee, without any need to

taste, though some drink their own: one, maybe two meagre
palmfuls until we end, at a loss in the badlands—it has to go

somewhere, you say, surfeit nutrients shed, musk of asparagus
steamed at night, the salty butter-melt running down our chests

as we feed each other, the residue handy for later, who knows
what we may run out of long after the Hasty Mart has closed

bodies of water, bodies of steam re-engineering the industrial
revolution from all opposing sides, east and west opening up

the wilderness, one dark tunnel after the next blasted through
mountains we love, the hallucination of a river rearing below

our berth bucking us, bucking us, for whistle stops miles past
the last spike and Roger's Pass, the body a round-trip ticket

along watersheds loud and wily beneath sheer glacial heights
to ever more roughshod tidal bores, the excess expelled after

but not our anger or the desire to be full: pour me another shot
of water, cowboy, we've got lots of time; you're holding mine

now and the mirrors we never forget about run slick with steam.

Runoff

What we release into the river.
How we alter the current.

The irrigation dam on the Old Man flooding the sacred

lands of the Peigan who have lived
here for generations on the arid Alberta plains.

The salmon ladders.
The transmigration upwards

slowing on the other side of the mountains, fewer
fish ascending waterfalls now absent.
Hydroelectric

dams everywhere in the middle of
nowhere: an invisible
sustain

able environment we sell—bill
boards defaced at the gates of Banff National Park

> *Don't embitter*
> *Don't starve the bears*

The town beyond Bow Falls
exempt from official remorse so it can

fence in more: tourists blind to

the missing wild

currant bushes we trans
plant from roadside
ditches along any highway climbing into the eastern

slopes of the Rockies, the civilized
currants boiled
in treated Elbow River

water, sugared and cooled

cellophane sealing in a tamed
alpine savagery
as lovers we grow

to forget the moment we taste it—
this confusion

of *currants* and *river water*
tartness
and *intent*, words

picked from the disturbed bushes and erased
of meaning in the 'natural'

flow of discourse, *It's good for you*

embossed on the empty
jars, sterilized or thrown away, cluttering
basements hungry for some purgative Boy Scout bottle drive or else

they are

dislodged from the landfill site during runoff
in the spring, residual tang mixing
with dioxins

piped up tendrils
of marsh weed and exhaled through the gills
of the jewelled trout we land downstream from the syllabic overflow.

III

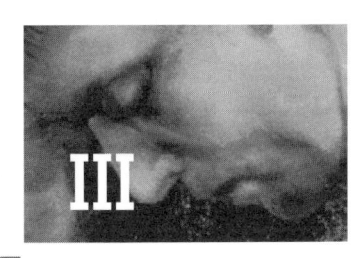

NARRATIONS

In the House of the Present

I rise through the house, your dog at my heels curious ears pitching forwards as we climb landing window angled open, stairwell hazy with the intense light of his barking as I enter time's leaky vacuum, having not come to visit in years, the hall dividing rooms not everyone finds his way into, the way through coming back to me, our parents still downstairs long after we are meant to have fallen more deeply asleep, dwindled voices ghosting me as I climb our fathers staring into their ryes and water while our mothers, so contrary, settle on how best to set the table in the English manner few pay heed to, silver against damask, carving set poised on crystal knife rests—how they come to sit next to each other on the Jasper Avenue bus, what in the 50s makes them start talking neither of us tries to guess at, our sisters at play in the aisle, transfers made to points far beyond the unexpectedness of our bodies, two sons born two years apart, your mother bathing you in the sink, skin pink against shining porcelain until as you crawl up behind me I step back our eyes downcast and lifting, meeting as I glance over my shoulder, small foot squashing smaller fingers into the Kashmiri carpet's deep crush as, pulling at threads, the sun bleeds through the clouds—what clouds—there always seem to be clouds as I look skywards, unfurled bolts of cirrus shading my eyes as slowly they open to what we wake to hours before anyone else your father in the eternal early light making us breakfast, bread trimmed of crusts set to brown in residues of bacon grease, he says, to fatten us up—to what other purpose does anyone cut into such yolks, two runny cow's eyes running across the countryside breakfast china I find misidentified pieces of in second-hand shops your mother's voice turning down the hallway with me until I open the door, blocks scattering across the plain of the floor, the blown-apart cities of the imagination no one ever moves into, cities built on the unlit side of the moon before you disappear ahead of me out the open window with your camera, the case discarded on the grass—there are still more images, still more destroyed cities in your head to set loose your mother, as she dies, anxious for me to set them free with you, but older, imperceptibly we live in atmospheres too heady for you or I to detect while in the closet hangs the silver space suit she one day makes you, the lucent helmet you wear when I come around clouding with your breath, though for now this sham orb glows, clear and hollow on its briefly exposed shelf, your dog clawing at the loose-woven rug ragged by your bed, coiling into a sleep none wakes him from until I am found in the kitchen where our sisters dry the last of the remaining day's dishes, clean faces caught in the plates before they are packed into crates, vestigial steam distorting the windows, and me wanting to wipe it away, wanting the two of us framed by the sill, framed and held by the willow where you sometimes read with your father among branches spreading low into twilight under the sweep of sun-gilt leaves we play unaware his book is closing, the most frayed of catkins sifting down onto our heads, neither of us ready yet to know what this house might make room for and what it cannot, both of us giving so little thought to our growing capacity for inattentiveness or to our called-out names

The Strata

deep below night we voyage towards the centre
of the Earth, descending from this house aligned
and remote at the magnetic heart of an orchard
Lake Okanagan mirrors, its sun-warmed glacial
cobalt leaking into a rift cut between the Tertiary
and the Pleistocene, your three sons absorbed
in a game, turned away from how I observe them
keen and cross-legged at the veranda's margins
stilled, no one else but you with a mother's heart
sounding, in the ivied layers of distance hanging
down in vines between us, my clear discomfort
as they sink an enemy's worth of glued plastic
frigates in your wash tub, its shallow waters astir
with breezes lifting airless from the Monoshees
those dusty, piss-yellow mountain flanks worn
down in the arid heat, the Battle of the Atlantic
rewon in August 1968, my undercover apartness
an aftermath of the cold wars boys wage on slow
summer days, my father stalemated, sick upstairs
powerless to drive me away across the Kicking
Horse Pass towards the levelling, scorched plain
of my birth, to mother and sisters and the sweet

cultivated earth I grow out of, its vast horizons all I know, a rogue disc in his back ready to slip the lasting wound of his war torquing the Pacific plate far beneath Vancouver Island's mysterious weight, the HMS *Glorious* sailing within perilous range of your sons' zeroed-in inch-long cannons

※

peaches, halved, and eased away from their dark doubtful hearts, culls gathered after the repeated falls in the orchard, delicious yet hours beyond sale, bruises rising too soon to incautious skin too many of us afraid to crack open their closed hearts, wary of the suspect reservoirs of cyanide within—so: while your husband prunes back the fruit trees' complacent arms, while my father turns in agonizing sleep and your sons shower before stepping out with their girls, we gorge upon dripping, hollowed hemispheres of flesh as, from inside your living room and deep down through its charred shale fireplace, we climb ropes unwinding towards the most aloof cavities of the Earth few seldom visit but dream about descend through expired vents in Mt. Snaedfells on Iceland, not far from the Pole, James Mason funnelling us through Vista Vision via *Academy Performance*, Earth recast in every cataclysmic rote special effect of the 1950s, Mason's igneous Prof. Lindenbrook unenamoured, not prepared to fall for unstable musings on evolution aired by his nephew Alec, recreated by a petrified Pat Boone, with Jenny, the youth's irritatingly frilly fiancée, trailing skirts after as, together tethered they wind down through the evacuated shafts lava cuts through strata of an almost seamless geologic record or, later still, when they set sail across a subterrean, shoreless ocean on a raft of fossilized wood, they discount every settled theory only to flee giants who too quickly shrink down in imagination to become our ancestors all bones reduced to merest show in a museum and worlds away from your house looking over a lake where Ogopogo surfaces through the chill hierarchies of time, blunt, scaly head breaching human logic, rising above everything I am able to see and sense so tiredly in a stranger's house oddly solaced by halved peaches you re-centre gently by freeing their tainted hearts, thick juice

dribbling down my chin, a boy near the verge
trapped between fathomless layers and attuned
to a spiralling inward journey torn from a star
barred ionosphere by the antenna on your roof

※

the Battle of the Atlantic, widespread and static
strategically at an impasse as my father dances
you across the floor, handing you to his young
co-pilot, both eager to take you for a first turn
up into the air in a Moth, your photo of the two
friends pinned above my desk while they try
to bargain down the man who owns this open
cockpit biplane, you looking through the view
finder as you readjust the lens before climbing
in, unaware at the controls my father's friend
is the one you are to wed, the runway dropping
away as you try not to resist such an inscrutable
pull from the Earth's centre, flying to the edge
of sensing what pulls at the heart, that far-flung
day weightless among the thin clouds striated
over the eroded precipitates and terse volcanics
of the Avalon Zone, the skittery craft retracing
the shadowed greys in Northumberland Strait

when it banks landwards, never to touch down
though of course you land and years afterwards
you bear three sons grown tall far from Moncton
in this lake-filled seismic rip where a continent
first attempts the stars, the years since nothing
but another of Earth's thin atmospheric layers
exact as the afterimage of an ancient oak leaf
fallen into a swamp, then alchemized to rock

⁂

the man who lends the Moth I cannot forget
however missing his face is from your hastily
composed snapshot, his features blanked out
by my father's shoulder as he turns unsmiling
from the hazy background, standing in the way
of the man whose regard might lift towards me
across unseen years, with whom I can someday
bargain, or to another blank-faced man like him
urge him to lift me from the Earth, high romance
our airplane veering so near the sun a prototype
both of us its pilots and its test, now precarious
between thrust and drag, learning how to ride
the thermals free from the disruptive geologies
below, every visible strata holding, withholding

till we are elucidated by the airplane's puzzling
abrupt crash to earth, all our details randomized
our humanity withheld at once by what little is
left, the blank-faced man lost to me, abandoning
me to the enigmatic bone shards of a story few
dig up, his high-flown body my father's broken
in a distant war, hanging fire in the afterglow
of longing's botched fuselage, his back twisting
turned to rock, illegible under time's cumulation
his heart preserved as beaten in my amber flesh
a dragonfly caught and for half-lives inert, toxic

※

that the details are inaccurate, that the movie
abandons the book is never the story, that old
Lidenbrock from Hamburg, not Lindenbrook
from Edinburgh, never stands still at the centre
of the Earth, but turns skywards with Alex not
Alec, his fiancée Grauben unlike Jenny, patient
waiting at the surface—*May God guide you*—
is not the story, though stories in the Earth may
connote passion to others besides geologists
Precambrian Silurian Devonian Carboni
Ferrous Triassic Jurassic Cretaceous Eocene

Miocene Pliocene Pleistocene Holocene
love catalogued by the arbitrary chronologies
imposed, by the ways our lives stratify, we fear
when glimpsed after the fact, what we live not
the story, nor what we later reflect upon having
felt at the time, though words leave us residues
and, with shifting fixed importance, shake out
atmospheres to sustain us, elements able to tell
us so little of our time on Earth, or of the Earth
itself, rock no less unsettled than Verne's multi
layered novel or any life—yours with a family
among orchards espaliered over the core; mine
cast down with the culls—metaphors of depth
vented from pressures released by any accident
of feeling resonant along our structural faults

❦

the man with the blank face is the man I love
photographs of our flight too in focus to look at
his features I forget, body enveloped in the rags
of volcanic ash I refuse to lift away, but daily
my heart re-spools in shaken handheld video
the final short walk we take down the Giant's
Causeway north of Belfast, miles from Canada

and far more haunted than we are: path thread
between Irish Sea and ruddy, green-crowned
cliffs where sheep ruminate in the salted grass
below Cessnas banking against the westerlies
jointed pentagons of basalt fused into columns
leaning or standing true all about us, their spines
thrown out by every erosion of water and wind
crashed against them, the history of the Earth
like us porous, so imperfectly exposed, body
spooning into volcanic body, frail promontories
picturesque over bays where, warped from rock
and wave, however rough, distant Vikings land
or fishermen weir salmon, my heartbeat's sonar
apprehending how near undersea creatures stray
ghosts breaching the surface, never the numbing
clarities of the sea itself, such deep mythic water
unfathomable, revising the Causeway's piled-up
stratagems while tides ebb, my heart unschooled
to portend how the blank man I still love would
far too soon cull and halve his life—his cleaved
heart petrified—every private mystery I scrawl
in embers across ceilings of stone to be misread
by all others who go spelunking through caves
descending through unseen gases to the centres

of their Earths, my story the fiction they guess might re-ignite their own—but I am incredible even to myself: my face impressed featureless by the inaccurate, accumulating layers of pathos

※

paradigms, strata, stills, the footage sprocketed through memory long after the TV switches off your sons re-scrolled in towels after they step male odalisques from the shower, afternoons of gunpowder hinted at, still, in the humidity draping them as they dry off and dress, forty years after the ultimate cruiser sinks, misspent plastic carapace bottoming in the stirred tin-pot Atlantic I ferry forwards in time with me, depth charges of the night after night I climb out from the centres of, ascending through the orgiastic dying volcanics of the love I compass my heart by, my dashingly stacked giants not yet worn to size, *who I am* forever an unfinished flight the unsettled boy I grow up from test-piloting the controls of a tiny single-seater zigzagging above the prehistory I would peel from my life in layers, but I am unable to land, my sad father kept isolated and anguished on his back, lucid with nightmares I madden with the antidote roar of my departing engines—while you watch me watch stereotypes voyaging towards the centre of some certainty no one ever shares, he senses the surfaces I impress form a record of blank faced men, though I suspect too few geologists of the heart try to rearticulate all the stories left dissembled under future layers—men tendered void—though other boys are made to believe history is held entire in the unending present tenses of these stratifications of ongoing love

Sombrio Beach

except for a screen of hemlock resisting sunlight
along the shore, they clear-cut this hillside tilting
in somersaults towards dazzled water, laying bare
the fragrant abysmal shade we cascade our way
down through, agile memory of a trail still slick
beneath our feet, slipping past lichened boulders
cedars toppling, midnight roots torn up by storm
breakers of birdcall and white noise spilling us
whole at path's end, oceanwards lured by excess
foam receding beyond pools the tides abandon

⁕

old growth hid from us once by a now lumbered
darkness in absence grows vivid as, wind-rough
ice-glazed and soil-eroded, we move unopposed
through narratives of light, the carnage of savaged
stumps, Cape Flattery cast adrift and comatose
across the strait, glare baring what we are loathe
to bear, grief and a love of the scarcely travelled
cheering us elsewhere, though every back road
returns us here, turns us towards the unexpected
exposed to sun and silence, sometimes to tears

The Troubles

until what centres no longer holds us, we compose pictures along the Falls Road, our car stopped shoppers window-gazing and unaware of the feints of shadow and light we insinuate among pyramids of fruit or trail across headlines in the newsstand tabloids as we jump quickly in and out, frame time with our viewfinders, the countless murals we snap drafted by sympathizers on the long overexposed exterior walls of the steep-roofed, red-brick, soot tarred houses, grocers, haberdashers, and hardware shops, murals about strikers who, two decades ago in Armagh, starved to death by choice, the English prison not far from the seat of my mother's family who left the North years before the Famine, later Loyalists settled in Upper Canada west of Kingston the first house standing still in the plentiful winds gusting over the lake and Amherst Island, its crawl space scooped from shale damp with the panic felt hiding with the family silver carried with care all the way from Markethill, Johnson's Yankee gang of sympathizers tacking across water, staging raids during what at school we labelled the Rebellion the unsettling climates trailed behind my ancestors becalmed into what is now a quaint four-poster bed and-breakfast where I would've taken you, another adventure in the *Boys' Own* story of Ireland we had hoped one day to expatriate, the history of two men who through their troubles unite as one, despite what might hold them apart, checkpoints and pipe bombs, this uncentred and sudden widening maze of streets turning us away from where we thought to go, visiting from elsewhere, driven by a friend who has lost any faith she knows where to take us so keeps us lost, hers an entire life of roadblocks and Guinness, having learned she is who she is where she is—the best and the worst—and, hoping to drive us clear of danger, turns us into the centre of a riot, the car dividing perspectives while rocks skid across a fragmenting windscreen, this woman at the wheel living in an eternal present that is not Belfast, her vision of this intensely passionate city a long-fallen capital where, despite every wrong turn, couples meet and love, where despite herself she drops us off so we can shoot murals to the dead mothers and their missed children—they shame her far more than they trouble us—these commissioned

vigilante works of art vitalizing the Easter Rising
and Civil War two storeys high in green and orange
or blacks and sombre greys in contrast to the coat
of arms painted by paramilitaries at every corner
of the Shankhill Road, the Red Hand of Ulster held
religiously palm-flat and forwards, complex URLs
of the UDA, the UUF, the UVF, and the UYM
blazoned in scrolls beneath crossed machine guns
and mute black-masked men who through torn slits
look at us while we block our shots, you filling up
your throwaway until it consumes itself, my hands
shaking, my Minolta unable to track however few
exposures my film still can make accommodations
for, both of us cropping similar photos of the same
wayside towns as we are later driven cross-country
on the grand tour, sheep-crazed and whiskey-wise
the kamikaze switchback roads along the jagged
coastline turning and turning us into unexpected
vistas, promontories sharpening against the azure
our separate records overlapping, as if something
untoward will drive us apart, a gesture or veering
look at a stranger, cognizant already of the troubles
we might import and give anxious voice to at home
love's terrorism, his sweet erasure so annihilating

it undoes the existence first of one of us and then
the other, the briefest of excursions across the most
faint of lines there is never any coming back from
the Republic a haven where the North goes to relax
the air on either side of the border acrid with turf
smoldering as it has for centuries in village hearths

Asymmetries

scuffed leather, a well-used brush, shod feet ambling from Monument a Colom to Plaça de Catalunya along La Rambla—sweltering languid—the promenade incinerating a wide swath shambling between opposing currents of traffic as salt on the stung breezes thins tonguing deeper inland, abrasive, yet intuiting a way through the throngs and between heavy fronds of succulent boulevard trees unmoved along this clamourous length as it hastens up from a wine-bright sea, whispering, damp air blown into my ear, solitary men and couples luxuriating in the sunlit cafés, itinerant cats asleep on ledges while a coarse brush loosens what time layers onto my shoes, my left foot wearied and flat, at rest on an old man's knee while he crouches in the unrefreshing shade I cast, this foot no longer very like the other after a clumsy break, its arch naturally fallen but shaped with plaster by a hospital orderly I am sure remains bent on artificial parity— the body in sync—a technician not caring

how his hands would unwarp me, one foot
dissociated from its unique hold on the other
though my estranged feet on the whole stay
perversely well matched, "a very classic case
of deformity," my doctor would say casually
my feet not once likened to Michelangelo's
David, my young body awkward above them
when he parades me about during professional
rounds, exposing my oddities without shoes
legs of my trousers rolled well past the knees
as the backs of his peers would turn from me
all through my childhood, authorities curious
solely about feet never meant to take me far
from home, to Barcelona, where an old man
rubs cream into dirty, scuffed leather, who is
like me, so used to indifference, to uncaring
Sunday crowds about him that as one person
pauses to browse gladioli, caged love birds
angel fish in jars before McDonald's—his
creams, hammer, and nails on bits of chamois
he spreads out, bald head bent to the task—
in deference never, but with an artist's passion
to fill and repair time—in Franco's aftermath
his fascism I would never know consciously

but I am very afraid I may still lust for, eager to search for balance and male beauty at odds with my own, my once matching shoes worn strangely and now wedged into unfamiliar pragmatic alignment when the old man props me in a kind of civic order precarious to hold without voiding my anarchy, his hammer tapping in my freedom of the city, chaotic streets walkable, leading me on, made mine at last and made melodious by the two half moons of steel he tacks into the black rubber heels I wear to blunt shocks past and future the oh-so-very-antique dust of this coastline expertly he buffs off, the light substanceless accretions of the endless afternoon I spare for Tarragona, an hour train ride to the south where in my mind I stand still, dazed in cool sun boiling off the carefully exhumed ruins of the palace of Augustus, its aching cavities soothed by light retained in the white robes of the Emperor's unearthly statue, an erect imperial presence long decapitated by progress while, just visible from the roof, the supine tumbled remains of an amphitheatre continue

sinking with the daytime moon's last quarter
into the azure fade-out as sea outruns horizon
all vanishings unceasing and the nearest I get
to history's blurring edges where time at last
breaks down into the eternal, an abstraction
I have no head for, like Caesar, my construct
for time less and less physical in this topos
where all things stop seeming so faultlessly
real, disinterested, eroded by what some call
passing, the sun-caught, slowly settling dust
a hallucination ambiguously caking my shoes
whatever few specks of it the old man misses
he suspends between pellucid layers, beetles
caught in amber, minutes or millennia, atoms
split, the frayed lace in my shoe perpetually
undone—and putting aside his brush, he reties
it, a part of the service in this modern city
where Ferdinand and Isabella, in a shadowed
medieval square, are still receiving Columbus
returning from the unknown where an entire
consciousness is born, the sudden arrogance
of its newness out of alignment with the old
its ignorance *in extremis* of what has always
been here, a world in conflict, kept in aching
imbalance, the extrinsic so exotic to anyone

who, mystified, comprehends little, myopias reversed or not by crossing over to sites felt once to be too far away or too used up to be noticed, the old man's brush suspending time in the air, the unsettling dust never properly the property of anyone—down to their corned toes, my feet so inarticulate no matter how delicately the ankles are hinged, these bones shards of marble someday to endure erosion with or without the deep subjective comfort of beauty, this sad lack of symmetry bearing down on my mortal soles, my fallen arches never to be golden, the body in promiscuous ruin and lounging in a chair while I leave off from admiring the lopsidedness my feet give shape to in leather, what time is left to me in this city, I spend among the moving crowds on the heels of lovely couples in Barcelona men who are my unstable present, their feet no longer oppressively held in such arresting relief by worn-out sandals as they walk hand in-hand with whomever they love—the only history I own up to is what time lives through this transience, this misalignment, this shine

IV
HYMNS

Excerpt from a Travel Journal

Arms folded across your chest, you stand before a window streaked with dusk.
Unlike me, you are not forever checking the clock turning its wheel of hours.

You don't need its hands to remind you we are waiting in what for you is only
one more station of departure. I thumb through my dog-eared train schedule

while you absorb more light by reflecting upon that window. From where I sit
your face shines, cast adrift in dust; I slouch in spectral outline. Is abstraction

trained on me by your haunted eyes or, as I write this out, have I truly started
to be erased? Our companion sits beside me, touches my arm: a young father

he's observed from afar just awoke and is on his feet, his straw-haired girl teasing
matches from the pocket of a man asleep on the bench next to ours, his raincoat

saturated in light drizzled down through the station's cloudy, faux-revival dome.
Our companion laughs, picks up the child, returns her, the matches, to the father.

Would you care for a light? Earlier, he'd espied an ashen cigarette dropping
from the man's long nervous fingers. Back beside me, he confesses happiness

might be found in the moving, avuncular rhythms of the father's hips. He lounges
eyebrows arched, smirking while you persist in being reversed in what he fears

is the fallacy of windows glazed opaque. His arm rests across my shoulders
one shivery squeeze and my attention veers, struggles to retain focus as black

ink runs hot across a now emptied page. So here we are, men who travel
in disguises we trade amongst ourselves, comedians in the same desire.

Masked in one, we are forever at odds with some better self the others wear
never sure which one we could each make our own: the one who embraces

the one who reflects, the one who inscribes—the kisses, panes, and syllabics rerouting, waylaying with equal dispatch wayward time. I recheck the clock.

Weeks ago we bartered the fickle identities imposed at birth. We have chosen to forget where we had met, how, why, exactly when. No matter. We appear

to arrive on one train and board the next. The hobo moon we sling over one of our shoulders stays wrapt in the edgeless handkerchief of day and night.

Eros

with apologies to John Le Carré

The man who comes here I have not met. He seems to arrange
to be at home when I am absent, I should accept that. The fine

dust of his muddied, transitory footprints I sweep up afterwards—
we would leave no trace, though little can lift the drips of coffee

rorschached into my bruised maple floors, an unscrambled code
zigzagging me to cups crumpled in the trash. Neighbours hint at

apprehensions of a shade behind my sheers who keeps appearing
to observe them. Where is he from? What persists to entice him

back, what does he overlook? What bookshelves and unfinished
letters has he left for later to nose a way into? Do my fresh-hung

shirts long for him to slip one on? He could be my stature. It may
be his contour I punch out of my pillows at night, his humid fish

scent rising from these dishevelled, test-pattern sheets, toes haired
unlike mine flexing past the mattress edge. Does he get up to take

a long ruminative leak before leaving and, sitting or standing, leaf
back numbers of *Foreign Affairs* jumbled on the tank? Can he lose

track of himself and the time, dick lazing between his thighs, slack
listening device? What besides the water dripping is there to tap?

Are his eyes clear? Skin soft, hair red—is he desperate for a shave?
Who does he work for? Is his toned intelligence acute enough?

Is what he might see mirrored in my bedroom window at twilight
something I could never reflect on at dawn, ducking the currents

in the river, its pink surfaces, no one else awake? Will he fight off
whatever ghosts him or will I be overcome? What about his chest?

Him

after Ron Mueck's Dead Dad, *mixed media, 1996-1997*

There is no rhetoric in an open mouth, the lips caught
mid-breath, nothing left to expel, his last few rasps

caught in my ear, a moth against wind-rattled glass
as dusk grew silent, the perpetual thrum of traffic

unheeded, no pulse. He was a man who grew small
in my eyes, how else could I remain a non-believer

until his features petrified into a mask no one lifts off
chin canted downwards, eyes stoppered into unscanning

ellipses, his pajama redundant, an inscrutable shroud
—if this is love, I have learned it too late: nothing stays

private when hands are held with the dead, my life
leached out, evacuating queer ethers into his body

denying rot in the final moments of touch, my face
wiped of awareness while, in lamplight, his continues

as life-like, hair unbrushed, skin wanting soap, jaw
clenching, gaze thrown askance. His was another self

the co-pilot I could never betray for men I have known
men secretive as he was about an invisible set course

gone nowhere now, time dumbstruck, a presence felt
its flight path the body erases, stalled among bedclothes.

10 Lines for X

with apologies 2 C. P. Cavafy

4 a decade I have been a10tive 2 memory—your body not 10ebrous
but backlit & smooth, 10 toes & 10 fingers itemized, multiplied by 2

my hands & feet bracing yours—this 10acious architectural recovery
of touch interlocking, wide-angled & true, squared off by the oblong

well of your bed, scared flesh 4ever 2 10der, cur10s drawn shut, 10dons
pulling both ankles 10se as you would arch 2 fast above me, 10tative

eyes turned askance, the 10 lilies I counted in a vase on your table not
open as we ate, the 10ure of our ½-built 10ancy dropping echoes voided

by your death, our 10uous quotient of nights never wholly quartering us
why else can I not 4get: your room's vacancies 10dered me numerate.

Way Finding

This is the blueprint I have been given, its lapses
its language: I locate myself on the second floor

of your house on D Street while you show me
the way you want to redo it, your vocation still

unrealized from basement to loft, though an ex
lover's cats have run of the halls, dispossessed

of rooms where no one appears to live through
the week I am here except to sleep and excrete

trailing after you down flights of stairs by closed
doors for our first morning coffees after a shower

and attempts at love we improvise in a makeshift
bed, bivouacked in the front parlour, your room

on the third floor stripped to the studs, the walls
months from plaster and a longed-for move back

in, restoration of your dream life spec'd in phases
CNN turned on in the kitchen, the anchor recasting

network variants of the same abruptly diffused
bullets of text, reports on Kosovars—or are they

Afghans?—expelled from villages over six times
an hour between commercial breaks, they score

the white noise I exist in with the cats in the air
cooled corridors of your late-Victorian row house

fretworks of wrought iron gating its arched, sand
blasted entrance, a city laid out from your barred

door not quite as L'Enfant would have drafted
but with all the symbolic might his street plan

could unscroll: a war-razed capital, his frontier
icon of power majestic while, outside redrawn

borders or high in the mountains, thousands wait
in the rain, their houses abandoned yet still real

to them, if looted and burned, each newsflash
eclipsing the one previous until I seem to cease

watching and, in the quiet, feel only what I feel
a Formica table caught between us while you sit

disoriented, a tall man with a stoop still inclined
ascending ahead of me storey by storey past ever

more sun-crammed rooms of your house, to figure
the path you blaze can't fail to dawn on me as self

evident, once through enough to apprehend a way
into your life, keys shiny under chinks in the terrazzo

the doors tried by a future phalanx of solitary men
till one unlocks, the room it opens onto appointed

to accommodate more than a transient occupying
space, the doorknob turning in his hand long after

those without shelter return to remake their homes
forgotten, for good or ill, in a country unknowable

from what newscasts expose us to, dusk collapsing
through stained glass in the hall skylight as we step

outside with my suitcase, faint sun bringing blood
up in the refinished floors while you reflect on how

far Washington's tree-lined grand thoroughfares
and side streets should steer us towards and away—

such is the compass of your power—I am no good at
displacement, space has a lexicon too many deform.

Fucking the Minotaur

In and out of light-denuded, ill-connecting rooms no bleaker than cells
never enough of us loined in towels scant as negligees swaggering past

doors with ravenous fatality; avid, incurious as—hirsute or logorrhoeac
elephantine or effete—we spiral down through a juggernaut of corridors

back upstairs, floor above floor below, the maze dizzying us into a raw
half-erect paralysis of longing—our eyes shifting, glazed flat—all flights

each hallway, every paint-peeling room never quite the alluring box hedge
of topiary figures the owners would like us to believe they have clipped

for us, where, despite any obligations we shed at the door, wary disparate
men might turn to other fresh men—love not a nightcap and recreation

but ardour, the basement bar not a refuge from sweating everything out
through pores in a dry sauna, whirling what's left away in the unchanging

water of the pool, only to travel goose-fleshed and powdered on the metro
the sober underworld of the city another homebound puzzle we would like

to dissemble, so look away when sullen eyes accuse ours, a game of bluff
minus the blindfold, every half-perceived acknowledgement one of denial

no less seductive, the slim anonymous flash of a stranger slipping between
passengers onto the platform, his sharp swivelling hips electric with a wet

sting of the towel snapped with malice from behind every shower-stall door
a gym-class revenant a few steps ahead on the escalator up into the snow

wind intent on goading us through an infinite grid of alleys until something
moves from behind a dumpster, such innocent hands annihilating our hunger.

Man of Your Dreams

He observes you come and go and remove your clothes, only to slip them
back on with wordless nonchalance, not even a solitary good-humoured

grimace between you four times a week as you knot your ties, part your hair
unnamed professionals as you go, divergent, into the fierce moon-sharp air

swimming in treated water barely cuts ice as you each ease into the shifting
lanes of divided thought, repelled as you kick beyond a shared and repetitive

privacy, lap after captivating lap seldom cooling, the salty concentration
undiluted by the precipitate bodies of faster swimmers—filmy fleet blurs

of Lycra, goggles fogging up, mists you roll snug inside towels to tote
home, hang dry with trunks shed on view: video in real time on YouTube

phantom outtakes of meeting every place, random tracks through snow
come together and suspended in a chilled embrace—man of his dreams

of his nocturnal emissions lingering at the slushy pool entrance, remain
where you are, a man without qualities, the abandoned stirred-up water

unreflective, not deep or shallow, anticipation as astringent as amnesia
or aphasia, anything you both could drown in should neither look away.

Our Embrace: Random Études, 1 Through 4

> *Sex is the last refuge of the miserable.*
> —Quentin Crisp

Pastorale

A ravine mulched with waste and tangled fallen
branches falling towards an unseen river and its

unseen rapids, you about to kiss me in the light
crystallized rain falling near the dead end of Daly

sun fading into the roadbed, the quotidian I might
before have too soon foreseen would fall in sun

spent mists about us now caught between freeze
and thaw, this unstable eclipsing hour I have brought

you to at once unromantic and unexpected, a quiet
cul-de-sac in a provincial city, fallow and domestic

not the falling nocturnal shade you long for, a lookout
high above the clear sweep of the silvered river

melting out of season in full moonlight where, a few
blocks over, you'd fall into a quick swoon and faintly

hug me, once: my body not Orion's, with the sword
you desire, but blunted by every constellation boring

you with unmythic pinpricks of what to me are cold
expanses between loosened stars, whatever might be

shared, if I were to believe in love, imperilled by harsh
astral velocities of your reckless falling spendthrift light.

Divertissement

Sex without kissing is all
about form, lips opened

for breath only, the unnamed
torso heraldic, the pierced

right nipple a medal of valour
untarnished by the tongue

face turned away as hands
work past hips, tattooed

skin of parted inner
thighs and buttocks a raised

map without relief of whose
sensate territory no one

can liberate, scrotum fanned
out above the perineum under

the about-to-flare lightning
head of a cobra, with no

lines to withdraw
behind, no matter how

deeply any are
hilted, pale

conscripts, eyes
closed or blank.

Pastiche

You slip in
side of me, a key in

side a lock
—a piano

key, a
locked jaw.

Caprice

Caught in two bodies lifted
from Klimt, ornate

autoerotic self-consciousness making
us kiss, gilt is

everywhere while we distract
ourselves—nothing between us but

gold courtly pretence, romance
trailing us, tired and out

of shape, though of the two of us
you stand broad-shouldered and naked

under this diaphanous
surfeit of ardour, a billowing

jewelled robe you encrust
me with, on my knees and looking

upwards, its glittery mosaic abstracting
my lust into objective

beauty, so, though wanting men
you still remain a man: silent

and untouched—
love a shroud quilted

from remnants—handkerchiefs
Liberty ties, sports

attire, Armani shirts—art
for art's sake, your athlete's body

unearned from labour
and without function, a muscled

exemplar of obsessions I am
disposed to admire, lips

poised as you hold me
in your sculptural

arms, my thin unworked-out
yearnings squeezed

so tight my head thunders star
eyed and blank, every unutterable

valedictory inside me
fast passing unremarked

upon, a sad Eden happily stale
mated by guile and artifice.

Warhol

with apologies to Wayne Koestenbaum

Hey there, Drella, it's me, Juan Baton: I erase you; I make you live—
the rod I rule with, diseased but social; its potency, prior to factory recall

an inflatable function of my body stilled, a balloon subtitling the freeze
framed, yawning torture of your films, my screen test becoming butcher

with time more shaved and tasty, a beefy snuff movie I am starring in
drugged-up, dazed, and odalisque, my cock a colostomy bag worn full

frontal and voiding desire, my insides all over your outsides, a loudspeaker
between my legs narrating blow jobs, no longer a microphone sucking

up passé modernist inhibition as it might have once, genteel and hidden
love then allegorical, asexual, allusive, now A-list, aphrodisiac, aphoristic

though, unlike you, I remain unAmerican, a foreign body, my ambivalent
alien destinies manifestly suspect and pissed away, but, hey, did I tell you

I aspire to baldness—so omega, so B-film, to be unwigged-out as you are
not, balling without tears, this kleptomaniac run-on sentence a time capsule

boyfriend after boyfriend after boyfriend after boyfriend after boyfriend
after boyfriend after boyfriend after boyfriend after boyfriend after boy

friend I lay end to end, the unmourned outlines of their flesh a compulsive
silk-screened orgy so empty and repetitious only the brillo-box scruples

of a museum could contain them—else no one will—longing contemporary
and unnarcissistic only in retrospect, the commercial properties of legs

and chests made abstract, dreamy citizens gone art-historical, devoid of life
RFK assassinated the day after Valerie shot you, his fifteen minutes almost

cancelling out you both, her anger no more notorious than your shopaholic
instinct to create, cannibalizing anything in sight, your scarred body a work

of the imagination I truss up until the lonely end, this breathy parasitic line
a film spliced with commas absent from your posthumous diaries, my own

angry voice made to slow down syllable by syllable, frame by jerky frame
as I project myself across the ready-made screen of your fame, ejaculatory

in homo slow-mo, a low-fidelity money shot so orchidaceous you organza—
a deadly improvisation you exteriorize stroke-free over my cropped-out face.

Portal

Drop the bombs, I say, *drop the bombs*, stand inside the portal
with your mother and hold your breath, your left hand in hers

while the house begins to shake, Ghats of the Indian Air Force
cutting low across the border, an escort to the French-built

Mystères about to strafe the airfield outside Multan, ancient city
of your distant childhood in Pakistan, but you are too young

to know the Sabres stationed nearby take flight too late to block
the raid, holding your mother's hand while dishes in the cabinets

clatter, the door jamb fixed above your head square and tense
as your shoulders, my hands smoothing, loosening the restrained

muscles of your back as you start to talk, *drop the bombs*, I say
drop the bombs, your heart opening, ten years in Canada, amazed

no one before me had ever asked, the first of your wars decades past
eyes askance, right hand grabbing mine in vestigial panic, no answer

when you call Karachi, Ramadan over, your parents at the mosque
the moon's crescent scything a quick, bright swath through the stars

as it arcs inexorably towards us across the unseeming turbulence
of the Earth, meteors raining down timeless windfall, an ice storm

we watch approach from the east, standing on your balcony, the last
Boeing 767 to lift away from the airport banking overhead, the Arctic

air close about us while, breathless, you long to take flight, not from me
or the knowledge of who you are, but from the peaceable coldness

of the north—no one way to pilot this shifting jet stream even your mother
might, fast or feast, hope is love—*drop the bombs*, I say, *drop the bombs*

hold my hand or let it go, neither of us either stateless or desperados
these words a portal without imprimatur to grant you safe passage.

A Boys' Own, with Queen

Up the valley the locals call you the lads, never ask after wives and kids
when you pull in for milk or gas at the general store near the crossroads

driving from the city every weekend from early April on, for three years
arriving in the summer before heat condenses in a sweat over weary farms

your new truck flush with fauteuils scavenged from back-road dumps
along alleys from Renfrew to Osgoode, claw-toed couches you recover

in period chintz, a chaise longue scarred and crammed among bedding
plants and stucco—every rococo touch should get the township talking

the schoolhouse languishing for thirty years after the province rethought
how it wanted children taught—and where—no longer in century-old

dowagers presided over by normal-school alumnae who too soon would
become engaged, the bricks past their prime, collapsing among the lilacs

and broken swings when you took it off diocesan hands, another couple
bracing for transformation in spite of the numberless repairs you fear

from loft to cellar, repointing the stone supports, fresh-adzed cedar shake
taking days to hammer in place for generations of weathering to tranquil

greys still ahead of you, the septic field to be laid next spring, running
water at last and hydro (locals shaking heads from afar), the one room

inside squared off by communion rails into cells for cuisine and sleep
each of you ceding a separate peace to cramped, intimate space, joking

men your age won't miss a family room, but crave a library for merged
first editions, the parish records painfully assembled about to be ordered

into a summation where you fit, and fit you will, within rural histories
less disposed to write you out—meanwhile you are last seen hanging

Pope Leo XIII repatriated in full regalia from the detritus in a shop
of long deconsecrated church antiquities, his tarnished frame filling

once sacred space, a light rectangle ghosted against sooty plaster above
the blackboard just left of the shy early likeness of a queen whose eyes

look down upon you uncomprehending, not because she won't realize
who you are, but because she is not yet a widow and still feels young.

Sandy Hill Gothic

The house down the street where we hope to live sells before
we have a chance to make it ours (the red-brick bay of chapel

windows cool at night until a fire is laid in the living room, olive
and mustard balustrades leading down from the front veranda

at sunrise to raked gravel and tended beds, the lawn given over
to daylilies and columbine, maples leafing shadow on bed sheets

beneath the mansard as we wake to a light breakfast, then work
in separate sky-lit studios where I adjust the scattered record

language makes and you revise key homeopathies for the newly
born and the dying) the house standing empty now and in wait

for the belongings of unknown others, most other houses not quite
as perfect, though never once do we peer inside, walk by apart

or arm in arm (glimpsing floorplans through undraped windows
with ample room beyond the hand-blown panes of glass for all

we own or hope to buy, knotted rugs and tactful prints, hardwood
unlikely to call for refurbishment) not afraid myself to continue

looking, with my hands make real what cannot be (imagined)
acquire a long occupied house others overlook, the yard gone

to seed on some untrafficked street, a structure less grand but in
want of repairs it could take years to find our way into, its shifts

in light we may guess at, where poetry and healing might intersect
with space enough for gaps always pre-existent (and halls connect).

HYMN

with apologies to G. F. Handel

Since he left him, he has been cleaning for days, suspending the dust
collected on every painted surface, its grainy near-transparencies once

too easily seen through and ignored, long unmoved cups and saucers
marking time in the kitchen cupboards, the emptiness the plates expose

when lifted, gaping—*agapé*—his sponge obsessive, his hand's abrasive
sweep wiping away what otherwise would fill in quickly, memory upon

unsettling memory surfacing of the untidy man he wants to forget
the man their time together changed him into, the man each hoped

a lover could stop him sliding back towards: a misanthropic archetype
observed lip-syncing *Messiah* as he jogs along in headphones to work

any mutual appreciation for self-ridicule as slippery as the chequered
floor he wets with Mr. Clean, its mirror stripped of the mud tracked

across it, of the food spilled, of desire discharged, bodies sinking down
a wall below a clock, slow minutes elided by hands inside unbuttoned

shirts and trousers, along sternum and hip, losing track for all hours
of whose is whose—*him* or *him*—spotless linoleum catching his lazy

eye, a lacuna he reflects upon when, once askew, nameless emotions
body forth unbidden, his face an illuminated tile damaged among his

many tiles as he knees up from the floor with his bucket brimming
with recovered grit, only to sort through photos either might have taken

their intentions in hindsight not forcibly posed, impromptu light angling
over his brain's pan of solvents, consciousness sponging up what he can

barely look at—the censure he inspired caught in the negatives still left
to print—though he files all forethought of the unknown life now going

on without him, a life he confuses with his own, his life promiscuous
however rearranged his surfaces or clean his drawers, the unclarifying

distractions of the body portentous in his downfall, the downfall
of his own body a matter of time, but thinking of the man who left

the accidental man come between them, the man he may yet become
it is impossible for him not to sing them unwashed hymns of praise.

Amnesia

The old man from Delphi cutting my hair trims holes in my thoughts
his own hair, he says, starting to thin during the last Greek civil war

holes you happen to step through at The Guys on Lembesi Street
within sight of the Parthenon, the ranks of columns reassembled

solid and tapered as athletes eight-across in a shower, a dazzling
relief in marble you walk from behind to lounge across from me

unrecognized with your boyfriend at the club's island bar, not stars
exactly, but swigging bottled Mythos with the rest of us, the other

celebrities signed, faded, and hung on the walls lovingly, the last
of the sunshine cobbled from the nearby streets slipping through

the entry unseen, a sweet anonymous boy who's unearthed the love
shared in the Metro under Sintagma Square, his heritage displayed

in glass cases on the platform while he smokes before perching next
to you on a bar stool and drawing my eye, my attentions not simply

archaeological, the boy as feckless and awkward as I was when you
met me, though he has a kind of unpolished candour, tall and Doric

his physique, with bits broken off, encountered at each astonished
turn of the Acropolis Museum, every shard catalogued to stand in

for memory instead of being memory itself, the boy not yet shattered
by love as he settles into a grin and his lager beside you, a man I still

don't recognize, a man I forget, whom I may have desired, our past
uncollective, a midden, fired vessels cast aside, never to have been

made use of, longing forever coiling inwards to be free of sentiment
beyond the agoras, the ruins isolated by gnarled olives and poppies

how to piece together whatever it is we want to efface, beauty recalling
partialities slipped free of, holes in our logic obstructed layer after layer

your lover putting a match to the boy's cigarette, columns blown down
at the Temple of Olympian Zeus, the cross-sections of marble spilling

across grass poignant as vertebra, views of Athens from Lykavittos Hill
rapturously spread, afterglow shed by the washed skin of a man's lower back

light chiselling my thoughts while in cuts fast as a hummingbird I lose my hair
in a barber's chair weak with whatever it is I can't forget and won't remember.

Days of 2004, Days of Cavafy

We Greeks have lost our capital . . . Pray, my dear Forster
oh pray that you never lose your capital.
—attributed to C. P. Cavafy by E. M. Forster

Away from the Houses of Parliament, wandering the streets of this ruined Confederation neighbourhood under maples loosening darkness along a river where men could linger

past midnight in the chill, late-season air, I am anxious, thoughts wandering through your far extinct quarter, not the squalid Alexandria you live in, but in the capital

you raise pediment by pediment at the rim of a great delta, city of golden arteries buoyed by the mythic reflux of the river where millennia of young men heroic first

in their beauty, in their loyalty to the body, awoke in each other's arms, exquisite fallen citizens true to the memory you keep fleshed out long after their city had abandoned

Anthony, long after your escape back from exile in Constantinople three years beyond the less than transient music of British bombardment, an alien philihellene loafing about

town randy if circumspect, a youngest mother's son slipping out once she could drowse only to muse past her death about the unreturned-to beds where after a game of cards you would lie with changeable lovers in the Attarine district, shirts and trousers too briefly shed, tattered, and for an hour revealing the wine-drunk gods your obscure city might otherwise have kept out of reach, unimaginable men, their genders you would redress years later make brashly presentable in a Greek so architectural, so arch in its pronouns.

❧

Forster said: you begin from within, a life doomed by its devotion to transient things youth, physical beauty, and passion—passion above all other: disreputable, excessive in the "Greek" way of life as you see it, your true self admiring men in the street unseen men whom you hope might still become and remain articulate in the artful, athletic tongue of your ancestors, those inattentively schooled sophists whose bodies as discus throwers adorn the coinage struck by adoring kings in commemoration of victories from Libya to Antioch, wars thrusting far across Persia into India, the whole of an ancient world inside you and you inside it, unearthed, the past intense with lust, the present imperfect with men like yourself or worse, fallen or raised poor, badly dressed, whose inglorious flesh so worn out by labour can still delight you, even in retrospect, however furtively

I look up to your second-floor balcony at 10, rue Lepsuis, where with a candle you sit into the dark hours revising, observing the infrequent clientele of the first-floor brothel

arrive and go, your eyes delighting in the girls, virtuosos of technique and the earning pleasures, a man in your forties guessing their names for no reason, your interest in them

idle: except by implication they never walk as others do through your poems, for down through the history of Greece you remake from chosen bits of marble you have stayed

enamoured with the endless debauch of young men who linger, depart from your city their desires voiced more often in the unseeming details you praise than in anything else

which I observe, though like you I am beautiful no longer, the best of your days like mine spent rising heartlessly up through the arid Third Circle of the Department of Irrigation—

who ever sees you, Cavafy, who follows, walking your deflowered city, this Alexandria where you have made all time simultaneous, yet seem always to despair of its passage?

❦

Amazing how any of us can persist at being in more than one place at more than one time sipping coffee in a bazaar while walking along a northern river gilded with brittle leaves

watching passersby, reliving the love we make with one man while at rest in the arms of another, looking up from a newspaper on a city bus to retrace your steps, you a poet

born two centuries back, your path hidden, however memorably you may have one night written about a man who years after your death might appear out of nowhere and act freely

from the study door I see you at work at your desk, yet I cannot see myself, a later man unknown to the city I live in, a city not any less imperfect than yours, a city like so many

with a disposition for violence, its young men after unaccountable days still found in bed with their heads bashed in, beautiful, naked, though there are times when men here seem

in appearance more able to act, citizens solemn, happy to observe men marry other men though by such public vows they become invisible, respectably move out to the suburbs

however ambitious their anonymity may be proclaimed in the high court as it overlooks the river and its currents, overlooks what might sink, what might get carried forwards new housing starts pushing the civic boundaries past limits not even you or I could have guessed, the men of every city made good citizens whom, sitting at your desk, you can

only envision as enviable devotees of pleasure—and they are, their self-induced beauty however VIAGRA-enhanced, used up as it can be in your time, though some of us hope

desire may be caught, its decline arrested long before it is gone, each man a taxpayer a contemporary Adonis constitutionally to be resurrected once a night in his own bed.

❧

There are times, as you know, when a city remains a room, fortifications thin as the walls street noises brought in on the coats to be shed, the weedy taste of the sewers on our skin

perpetual transients of the sheets, men from all over town inviting themselves in for an hour for the night, not here on approval, beautifully unmarriageable but candidates for coupling

and culpable of nothing but the sweet relief of disappointment, like-minded citizens unable to dissemble inside the room's time frame for long, skilled at keeping artful conversations

going only so far, articulately awkward, and knowing in their silences, the space of the room immediately transformed into the space in their arms, each instant instantly archival, the eyes recording unquestioned appointments—shelves lined with books leafed-through or unopened curtains drawn, chest of drawers randomly pulled out, narcissus dead in a glass on the night stand, double bed islanded under a soft-lit fixture, shirts unpressed yet hung, as they are meant to be, in a wardrobe—the air stale with memories no one is ever intended to know

though afterwards putting on clothes in the quick opposite order they were taken off standing at the door in our socks, closing it behind them, we find ourselves wondering

wandering the streets behind them to the outskirts, musing on what barred store windows they might browse, on where they likely stop for a beer on the way home, men we might

greet or ignore on the street for weeks afterwards, men who travel lives not too indifferent to our own, travelling from Sparta to Thermopylae, from Sussex Drive to Albion Road.

❦

Constantine, admit us: we all want to be Alexandrians, all want to be former exiles who stand elegiac on our balconies and observe the street, knowing the ruined glories we anticipate

in transit below are behind us not ahead, knowing vestigial greatness may now lie elsewhere knowing the cities where we live—any city—like Alexandria at last are enough, our attempts at mediocrity sufficient to construct an urbanity, a backdrop for a life, golden boys in our arms as irredeemable as those aging anywhere, as talented in excess, their inelegant candour found

foremost in the nerves, in the rapacity of their tongues, any unused callowness reworked later by the heart, residual bits of history excavated over time, a communal transcript none of us

ever knows entirely—anecdotes retold in every city, in every suburb, in fragments not unlike lifetimes you revise boldly, discretely, poems of a fallen city, of unchaste, eternal Alexandria

men of the future looking backwards as I look to you for a city map unfolding to relocate where you are and where I might yet go, a man who walks along a river below the seat

of power in an unhellenic, plain-spoken country where few can still imagine there are gods where I can pause along a lonesome street to give a stranger less unsatisfying directions.

The Afterlife

How my absence becomes their memory, how well they seem to keep it

those French men whose arms might have too recently held me, their fictive
vernacular coating my tongue, lying in bed together in the grip of a cold

my imagination a flu season as, in a fever, they navigate the demotic streets
of the Market without me, enthralling labyrinth of my prime I did not know

I was living, thankful too late, French men disposed by their genes to walk
fashionably dressed without umbrellas through unforeseen aesthetic frissons

of freezing rain, body heat stabilized by cafés americains and pains au chocolat
their Belgian-wool coats unbuttoned and soaked through, reminiscence cut

with half-and-half at the Bolangerie française on la rue Murray, yesterday's
English dailies yet to be trashed, the pages torn and open at my obituary

how little they knew about me, in retrospect, how little there remains to tell
the shape of me shaken from their sheets—but never the stains: unbleachable

lingering after the allophones whose lips they couldn't forget while we kissed
quit them finally, or the locals who still elude them, despite the exceptions

how fast and dirty they found my tongue, its grammar desiccating their skin
with prosaic western inflections of wind and mountain air, how they came

without prejudice or lapses in taste, how very quick I came to loving them
loving the claustrophobic wood-frame houses abbreviating the back streets

of Gatineau along the river half-thawed between us, the pigs' feet boiled up
at The Raftsmen, the sugarings-off, until the capital's opportunistic illnesses

overtook us, the sweatshop politics of desire quarantined by grande politesse
all of us made bilingual officiously, tendered inseparable, taciturn, and bored

so, courting temperatures, we would skate the wind-chilled canal in February
without scarves, the moon rheumy-eyed behind a gauze of jaundiced cloud

ungrateful the patches of thin ice we sought at Dow's Lake's centre never broke
open beneath us, dropping us into the eddies spring's onslaught would flood

algae-rank with E coli—wanting infection to render us deaf or incomprehensible
incubating consensus, hoping cold choleras of the heart might sicken us fast

carriers vanishing undiagnosed, perfectly past tense as expected and just as well.

V

Polygonics

Though you are afraid of heights walk with me along the breakwater
   its narrow double-jointed finger crooked straight across the flat

plane of the sea, mountains the sun cuts jagged against the distant
   shore turning as we turn, each windblown angle we negotiate

widening our perspective, pivoting us farther out than we expect
   stepping tentative along concrete poured high above the endless

verticals skindivers travel along below the ocean's surface, vicarious
   tangents you or I might fathomless have followed part way down

with other men, turning waterlogged back, amnesiac and gasping
   for air, intake lines tangled, guessing afterwards at wrecks we are

sure must list deeper still, literal and barnacled with what we let fall
   inadvertent, turning, slipping unnoticed through the currents past

waving skeins of kelp towards vanishing points few dwell beyond
   the lonely plane of the sea a polygon whose arbitrary shapes

alter as we zigzag along, the strait unhinging, bisected by migrating
   birds and Cessnas, tugs and kites, our faces briny with sun-shined

breezes, the extinguished navigation beacon a terminus where unblinking
   we stop at the vortex of deafening, unheard-of waves, not caring what

vectors may later point us elsewhere while we take in the fresh sweep
   of the horizontals about us: ocean, sky, and shore flat and thunderous

horizons dazzling as lightning shaken out in sheets, the breakwater
   the long arm of a compass projecting a direction for every line

across other lines, many lovers walking arm in arm with us or away
our arc ascendant, a half moon carrying us forwards unobserved

under open skies, geometries beyond the everyday plotted on the sea
you and I: both of us graphing possible trajectories of the limitless.

Acknowledgements

I would like to thank the editors of the following print and online journals where these poems first appeared or were republished, sometimes under other titles and occasionally in radically different forms:

Arc:	"Sandy Hill Gothic"
Bei Mei Feng:	"Anxiety," "Aquarium" (in Chinese translation)
Canadian Forum:	"Anxiety," "Man of Your Dreams"
Canadian Literature:	"Polygonics"
Capilano Review:	"The Troubles," "Days of 2004, Days of Cavafy"
The Chiron Review:	"10 Lines for X"
Contemporary Verse 2:	"Ideogram, in the Half-Light," "Geology of the Body," "Persona," "Hallelujah," "Free Associations," "This Land Is Our Land"
The Danforth Review:	"Installation in Homage to Gathie Falk," "Aquarium," "Runoff," "Divertissement," "The Troubles"
Descant:	"Fucking the Minotaur"
The Drunken Boat:	"Days of 2004, Days of Cavafy"
enRoute:	"In the House of the Present," "Asymmetries"
Event:	"Eros"
The Fiddlehead:	"This Cabinet," "Frieze," "Our Embrace: Random Études, 1 Through 4," "Warhol," "Amnesia," "The Afterlife"
Grain:	"Caught in the Updraft"
Lichen:	"On Evia," "Way Finding"
The Malahat Review:	"A Boys' Own, with Queen," part two of "The Strata" (as "Academy Performance")
Matrix:	"Shopping at Capers"
NeWest Review:	"Foul Bay at 2 AM"
nth position:	"Anxiety," "A Boys' Own, with Queen"

ottawater:	"Anxiety"
Peter F. Yacht Club:	"This Land Is Our Land"
Poetry Canada Review:	"Le Tombeau de Sylvia Plath"
Prairie Fire:	"Aide-Mémoire," "Inwards," "Aquarium," "Portal," "Hymn"
Prairie Journal:	"Runoff"
PRISM international:	"Him"
Queen's Quarterly:	"Excerpt from a Travel Journal"
Vallum:	"Pathetic Fallacy"
Windsor Review:	"Saumon Fumé," "Sombrio Beach"

Some poems first appeared or were republished in several anthologies and limited-edition chapbooks: *Vintage 95* (Kingston: Quarry, 1995), *Oxygen* (Maxville: above/ground, 1999), *Ten* (Maxville: above/ground, 2003), *Runoff* (Ottawa: Viola Leaflets, 2003), *Asymmetries* (Victoria: Frog Hollow, 2004, two slip-cased booklets, *In the House of the Present* and *The Strata*), *25 Years of* Tree (Ottawa: BuschekBooks, 2005), *Long Journey: Contemporary Northwest Poets* (Eugene: Oregon State, 2006), *Open Country: Canadian Literature in English* (Toronto: Nelson, 2007), and *Seminal: The Anthology of Canada's Gay Male Poets* (Vancouver: Arsenal Pulp, 2007). Above/ground press republished "Anxiety" as a broadside (*Poem* #192, December 2003).

"Asymmetries" and "In the House of the Present" won Second Prize in the poetry category of the 2003 CBC Literary Awards. "Days of 2004, Days of Cavafy" won Silver in the poetry category of the 2006 National Magazine Awards.

The epigraphs throughout are drawn from: *A Passage to India* by E. M. Forster (London: Edward Arnold, 1924); "A Kite is a Victim" in *The Spice Box of Earth* by Leonard Cohen (Toronto: McClelland & Stewart, 1961); *The Naked Civil Servant* by Quentin Crisp (London: Jonathan Cape, 1968); and "The Complete Poems of C. P. Cavafy" in *Two Cheers for Democracy* by E. M. Forster (London: Edward Arnold, 1951).

I would like to thank the following friends for their willingness to act as sounding boards for these poems during their often long evolution: Alison Beaumont, Rita Donovan, Robert Gore, Neile Graham, James Gurley, David Katz, Blaine Marchand, and Doug Schmidt.

Barry Dempster, whose keen eye as my editor spotted weaknesses these poems are much better without, helped me notice subtle areas of possibility to explore further and refine. I am also grateful to Maureen Scott Harris, Kitty Lewis, Alayna Munce, and Alan Siu for the care taken in preparing this book for press, for the elegant physical entity now housing it, and for every other attention they continue to lavish upon it. Thanks also to Diana Tegenkamp (and Holly Pattison too) for capturing me in one of my more bashful moods.

The following poems are dedicated to: "This Cabinet" (Jennifer Vine), "Caught in the Updraft" (Pam Barton), "Free Associations" (Erín Moure), "Installation in Homage to Gathie Falk" (Ellen Treciokas), "Aquarium" (Serge Duguay), "On Evia" (Mark Gallop), "In the House of the Present" (David Young and in memory of Margaret Young and Christopher Young), "The Strata" (John Edwards and in memory of Helen Edwards), "Sombrio Beach" (Neile Graham), "Asymmetries" (Gordon Dixon), "A Boys' Own, With Queen" (Blaine Marchand and Jamie Robertson), "Days of 2004, Days of Cavafy" (Neile Graham and James Gurley), and "Polygonics" (David Katz).

John Barton's previous books include *Great Men, Designs from the Interior, Sweet Ellipsis,* and *Hypothesis. West of Darkness: Emily Carr, A Self-Portrait,* his acclaimed third book, was republished in a bilingual edition in 2006. Co-editor of *Seminal: The Anthology of Canada's Gay Male Poets,* he lives in Victoria, where he edits *The Malahat Review. Hymn* is his ninth book.